Intimacy, Obstacles, and Miracles

Intimacy, Obstacles, and Miracles

Poems by

Jane Simon

© 2026 Jane Simon. All rights reserved.
This material may not be reproduced in any form, published,
reprinted, recorded, performed, broadcast,
rewritten or redistributed without
the explicit permission of Jane Simon.
All such actions are strictly prohibited by law.

Cover image by Lesya Nak
Author photo by Julius W. Cohn

ISBN: 979-8-90146-602-5
Library of Congress Control Number: 2025950113

Kelsay Books
502 South 1040 East, A-119
American Fork, Utah 84003
Kelsaybooks.com

*Thank you to my family and friends
for being here and there.*

*Thank you to my generous and patient poetry teachers
especially to Molly Peacock, poetry midwife.*

*Thank you to the puppy dogs in my life
who love unconditionally.*

Acknowledgments

My thanks to the following magazines and their editors:

Arizona Quarterly: "Grove Street"

Black Buzzard Review: "Everywoman"

The Breath of Parted Lips: "Stiletto-Heeled"

Columbia Poetry Review: "Basquiat"

New Voices: "Song of the Climacteric"

Poet Magazine, Eighth John David Johnson Memorial Poetry Award: "Song of the Climacteric" (Honorable Mention)

The Ravens Perch: "Fish Out of Water," "Muse," "The Entertainer"

Verse Virtual: "Street Woman with Red Blanket"

Writer's Digest, 18th Annual Poetry Award: "Ode to my Octopus Dilemma"

Contents

INTIMACY

Mind Lift	17
Everywoman	18
Odd Intimacy	19
My Stylist and the Iguana	20
On All Soul's Day	21
Scorched by the Torch	26
Stiletto-Heeled	28
Grove Street	29
Nothing But Horses, Day and Night	30
Magical Owl	31
Privileged	33
Bemused	34
Fish Out of Water	35
Spot on Earth	36
The Entertainer	37
Glass Rose	38
Basquiat	40
Song of the Climacteric	41
Ukrainian Woman	44
Street Woman	45
I Love to a Degree	46
The End Is an Entity	48

OBSTACLES

Near Escape	51
Marianne, the Octopus and History	53
Bombast	55
Thought Train	56

Itch of Impatience	57
Iron Grid	58
Repetition	59
What Game Is It	60
Octopus Dilemma	61
Elephant in the Room (or How to Hide a Big Problem in a Small Space)	62
Occupying Spaces	63
Being Ghosted	65
Sax Player in Pandemic	66
The Wolf Is Coming	67

MIRACLES

One Day	71
Circle Poem	72
Survival Miracle	73
Hurdle On	74
Hot Flash	75
Musician	76
In London-Like Fog	77
Better Self	78
Moments with a Leporidae, a Canine and Me	79
Daughter with Birds	80
Alchemist Artist	81
Pathway of Words	82
Impetus	83
Muse	84
Saving the Orchids	85
Common Sense	86
Expectations	87

Passing	88
Exit	89
A Meditation on Ruth's Cradle	90
Learning to Love the Old	95

*People need windows and mirrors.
Mirrors so they can see themselves
and windows so they can see each other.*
—Lucille Clifton

For me, poems are both mirrors and windows.
—Jane Simon

INTIMACY

Mind Lift

To lift the mind out of the mire,
I take a teaspoon of warm water
and wonder how it all came to be,
the origins of all of us.

I observe the animals
From the fierce dog to the iguana
whose throat balloons with grandeur.
I witness their variegated dances

as they live free of details.
I view the green-topped hills,
imagine climbing them fast
as I once did but the heart,

no longer young, sputters.
I turn back to admire the animals
who do battle with the seasons
who don't yield to the mire

who dare not surrender
to wild weather. The animals
grapple. Their behavior inspires
and I don't need more than their answer.

Everywoman

In my dream everywoman has a notebook,
canvas, easel and song pad. The boys surf
the flow in Mexico. The girls laugh
at the shore. Adults hover over the water.

In grandmother's long leather gloves
I creep my camera through my daughter's
bedroom. Dad handsome in red suspenders says
"silk, cotton, rayon, red is still

the color of the evening." Marianne is
the kind of woman who knows what
a dog thinks. We brag big brains
while cats and dogs won't wage war

and even though my major isn't music,
I'm invited: everywoman
needs a notebook, canvas, easel
and song pad in this strangeness.

Odd Intimacy

We fall into the quandary
of intimacy from our beginnings,
birth to death.

To be with oneself and to be
with another already engages (ensnares)
us in the quandary of entanglement.

Of course, we try to suppress (repress)
the continuous paradox of being
involved (independent) but some of us

Balk and some of us talk
in disguised phrases and some of us,
torn by the oddity of intimacy,

Occupy the beds of hospitals
where doctors and nurses
take over and we lose

(Abandon) control, body, mind,
soul. Intimacy can be
treacherous (rescuing).

My Stylist and the Iguana

I cart my loot from Trader Joe's along Columbus Avenue,
including a plant whose green leaves turn pink as they unfurl.
I find my hair stylist Woody leaning against a lamp post,
sunning himself and I am reminded of a green iguana basking
on a red clay roof like those I've seen on the island of St. Martin.
I am in desperate need of a haircut but I think I've camouflaged
the urgency with a headband that reaches from ear to ear.
But here is Woody and here am I, and we agree to undertake
the task. Once in the swiveling chair, a twinge of guilt races
through me. I've yanked Woody out of the sun. I think
of the iguana who spots some luscious vegetation and scampers off
into the shadows. Woody does the job like the expert he is,
each little hair now pruned and tidied into place and
I exit the shop with an aura of a perfectly manicured plant.

On All Soul's Day

For Al, November 1, 2023

Today is All Soul's Day.
Al passed almost a year
ago and I don't know

if he believed in the Soul.
He caught life on the ear
of an enigma

and I almost caught
the gist of his enigma. (I will continue
to try to sort this out.)

As a pathologist, he studied
death and the body of disease
but soon left the field and devoted

himself to jazz and playwriting
and projects and causes
like the nation of Sudan.

Why Sudan you ask?
Because a Sudanese person
asked him for help.

Al was my oldest friend
from the 1960s when we met
on the beach in Puerto Rico.

This island united us briefly.
We cherished the ocean
and the warm breezes

and the sound of the waves
beating the shore, and the lingo
of the island people.

Al found me, perched at ocean-side
as I scribbled poetry, dreaming I was
Buddha with my head bowed, buried

in medical textbooks, and
occasionally gazing at the horizon.
Al didn't say that I was crazy to think

I was Buddha. "Why not?"
he remarked. "Buddha is as good
as anybody else."

We were full of adventure,
and of music and Al tickled
the piano keys late nights

in the Cellar Bar in Old San Juan.
Afterward, the waves lulled us
to sleep as they lapped at Al's

door opening to the ocean floor
a few yards away. There was the sea
lapping, lapping.

On San Juan night as was the custom
we bathed in the ocean, nude under moonglow
embracing as twins in the womb.

How our lives darted in and out
like the wind for six decades,
like rivulets of water, here a wave,

there, a wave. Al wrote plays and acted
the part of a whimsical god who spoke
in riddles. His god was lanky

with gray-white hair and wore
a white business-like shirt
and sat behind a rectangular desk.

Al's god asked questions
and offered few answers but
agreed that man is the most

dangerous animal on earth.
More than anything, his god
provoked and riffed on

enigmatic tunes. Over years
of phone calls, we spoke about
the crazy universe and the lack

of solutions to the big questions.
So Al cupped his palms to catch
questions and answers

that dissolved in the salt
of rain and ocean water.
Finally, Al found love

with Maggie who accepted
his brand of intimacy and he
no longer wanted to travel but

didn't mind when Maggie took
trips to France to smell the lavender.
Al was now a home-

body, content to wander the sidewalks
of Manhattan until his generous
heart needed repair. And he rode

a rough wave, his body into the
auspices of the surgeon's office.
But sometimes medicine is only an art

and not a miracle-healer and now
I remember Al, musician-provocateur
and celebrate his life from beginning to end.

Scorched by the Torch

For Woolf (2006–2021)

A recent presence
is now an acute absence.
One hopes in a lifetime
for few such occurrences.

Loss is the word
I want to escape,
but I can't.
There is no exit

from emptiness
the hole of sadness.
To leave it somewhere,

anywhere. Dilute with drink
but the measure is too
temporary; I sink to the bottom
of the glass that is never deep enough.

The ache I can't reach.
The scratch that refuses
relief. I'm stuck

in this autoclave of heat
burning with the cold
scorched by the torch of love.

Stiletto-Heeled

I go stiletto-heeled
      the leather minis
           mothballed, the garters

a weeping woman, sleepless
      compost receding
           rage and sorrow

I like to think
      no harm comes
           to the animals

Spelunking dry and wet
      leaves on trees
           caught fantasy

Shepherds howl, dark night
      soul. In the fog
           I take no photos

Grove Street

Let us accept our loving, holding
a mirror to our faces, never escaping
as we climb snow leopard mountain
to completeness

Let us accept the lithograph of Braque's
religious stained-glass window reaching out
above us from your red brick wall
over log-filled fireplace with its
mantle holding Grove Street, tiny
antique windmill weathered next to
the photo of broad-faced Hemingway
in his fringed vest, your hero

Let us accept your fear of
Milwaukee, Wisconsin, your fear
of nothing less than nothingness. And Beckett
hovering weasel-eyed on your easel,
wrinkled like an old Greek olive,
whose lines become ours

We will wait for Godot
or love. What else is
worth waiting for?

Nothing But Horses, Day and Night

For Debbie

Today is someone's birthday. Perhaps today is the special day
of my school friend Debbie who adored horses. But I haven't
heard anything from her since our grammar school days when
she was whisked away from public to private school. Her parents
hoped this transition would lift her out of horse daze/craze,
her compulsive love, the need to sketch nothing but horses,

day and night. I could see Deb's point of view.
What else to dream about but prancing creatures to carry one's
body and soul over treacherous ground. Her parents wouldn't
buy a single pony but conceded to gift a dog, a brilliant red
Irish setter, a rare pedigree in Rockland County,
but one after the other was stolen from their yard.

Deb's parents threw her fancy birthday parties.
Her pretty mom was petite, pony-tailed and fair-skinned.
I could sense her chagrin in Debbie's proclivities
for blue jeans and horses. How she wanted another
kind of daughter. Perhaps, like me? But I could not
draw any kind of animal to save my life.

Today the thought arises from the deep recesses of years past:
how Deb intrigued me and how her mom suffered
because she wanted a different kind of daughter from the one
delivered. Perhaps there is nothing more
than luck? Nothing more than chance, the challenge
to accept what is gifted by the gods.

Magical Owl

For Barry, Central Park provocateur, a barred owl willing to preen his white feathers streaked with gray in the light of day.

Though owls are typically nocturnal, Barry makes regular daytime appearances, and has become something of a performer, seemingly unfazed by adoring fans and the paparazzi.
—*The New York Times,* Nov. 22, 2020, Metropolitan p.1

Safe pandemic pursuits
Search the trees for visiting
Avian Species

But owls? Their magical eyes
Is it fair to pursue their private
lives? Who owns what part

of our steadfast trees?
And who decides the ethics
of my probing eyes?

Peering and searching
for one of the 300 visiting
species that intrigue me

Trapped in a pandemic
Scrambling for outdoor
Entertainment

I search relentlessly
For novelty visiting
Our trees whether

Light or ominously dark
The flight of the bird
The plight of the owl

Is not easily understood
I project my concerns
But the owl's truth

Remains his own,
Mysterious,
Quizzically owl-y

Privileged

Let me riff on those 'privileged':
those fortunate enough to land
in the 'rich' or 'right' family

Remember the cliché
"Born with a silver spoon?"
There will always be

The privileged, though
neither you nor I
achieve that status.

No matter that with privileges
come possibilities as well as
unforeseen calamities.

No need to look further
than the Kennedys or Diana:
who'd want to be a celebrity chased

By crazies or the paparazzi?
Let me live content in the vicinity
of my undiscovered novelty.

Bemused

A bemused air allows for what comes my way
to cope with stray wings of insects, bats and birds
that sail, fly, perambulate on bellies like snakes
in all colors and shapes. Prepare is a word to
remember but not enough. Bemused
is the word I hope to use, to brave a smile
when lights dim or to toss a jangled head,
embrace the unexpected zing or cacophonous
ring from an old foe or beloved friend.

Fish Out of Water

Dad showed his interest
in us kids by clipping
articles from *The New York Times*

Clipping was safer
than kissing, or brushing
lips to cheek

The coelacanth, a fish thought
to be extinct was rediscovered
trapped in a fisherman's net

I envision his lunge
eons ago, from sea to land,
unwieldy body, sprouting
lungs and appendages

Like Dad, unmoored,
an outsider, searching
for his spot on earth

Dad, an odd fish. We
five kids agree, days
after the newsprint fades

Today I ask what drove
the coelacanth from the sea?
What spurred Dad to leave us, his family?

Perhaps it was curiosity that led him
to risk an unraveling, the long, arduous
journey to end in a dubious finale.

Spot on Earth

Didn't sleep well last night; kept thinking I should
        put socks on feet. But "I'm not cold," I said to myself.

"And maybe socks would make me too hot
        and then I'd wake up."

        But then myself said, "You missed the point!

The matter is not about temperature but about grounding.
        These pink polka-dot socks root you

to the planet and assure
        that you have a spot on earth."

The Entertainer

He is always proving to someone that he exists.
On the ship's deck,
        at the 6am breakfast
he aims to entertain the entire round table
of blurry-eyed passengers
with his whiskered joke.

Suddenly their eyelids lift
because the punch line is coming,
        sprinting around the corner,
outrunning the first cup of coffee
to win the race and fill
the passengers and the entertainer
        to the brim.

Glass Rose

Michael Rabin (1937–1972)

Shocked, I see you dead
on the autopsy table
assigned to me at the
Medical Examiner's office.

How does the pathologist
who heard your music
the summer of 1960
make the Y-shaped incision?

A rose at any angle
self-pollinating
red & green, blood-red
with your blood in a

Glass case of musicians
shattering so soon
on your polished floor
on West End Avenue?

Rabin, dark virtuoso
on stage of my childhood
God of Lewisohn Stadium,
God to me that summer

With Kathy, the historian,
playing her piano in a
collage of newborn babies
like blood red roses

From violin cases, playing
to rhythms of our minds, into
Beethoven's deaf ear,

Your tone strong, sweet, colorful.
Self-pollinating roses
peel & one more yields.

Saint Bach granted God
a grandfather lifetime
of music to his Glory
and you are dead at 35.

How do we use our trained minds
beating time with feeding spoons
knowing precisely how
to hold on, let go?

Basquiat

(1960–1988)

Painting white on black
fertile soil of self
drawing at three or four
eye's orb pumping
blood in black America

Halo of royalty
art's savvy
bird's star of bebop
ornithology and Parker
sugar, dope, tar skin

Marshals grip the skull
a crown of hero's thorns
in a white city
a Trojan horse across
John Henry's latissimus dorsi

This muscle man of steel
bows to a driven child
a leg kneels
a cool hand
to the Prodigal Sun

Stiff skull, scarred face
a dance break
a drummer's run
heads off to the king.
It is 1988.

Song of the Climacteric

> *. . . autumn can be long, golden, milder, and warmer than summer . . .*
> *the most productive season of the year.*
> —Germaine Greer

I'm the woman invisible
        noted for bad behavior, moles
grown a crone quintessential

A sad Parisian lunch
        lithe, young women
lionize silver-haired men

An unkind sunlight
        plays on puckers and sags
I shun short skirts, bright dyes

Cease to fret
        unwanted liberation
I nurture, I invent my own ritual

From fecund to infertile
        I stride the night
a cat rides my shoulder

No surgeon's scalpel
        I drop obsessions of breasts
shuck off scorn

Curse those who
        would bromide & blood-let
us of the climacteric

No boosted morale
        men leave Cher, Fonda anyhow
Plenty of company: two cats,

A thousand rabbits, seven geese
        I turn my gaze outward
on bountiful feasts

I'm not a dry leaf
        in the antechamber of death
my autumn warm, my harvest aglow

Human populations
        no longer choke
this minor theatre, my life

From star to wise actress
        agog and spellbound
I pass and savor

The music of sound
        sing of serenity and power
surmount pity's hold

Sun shines down prison's ego,
        crocuses poke
through glistening snow.

Ukrainian Woman

From a newspaper photograph

The white-haired woman
legs crossed under a long,
grey skirt resting above
her booted feet, roots
into rough, dry ground.

Behind her remain
the dregs of a bombed-out home,
roof splintered, windows
heavy-lidded, like eyes
assaulted and blinded.

Her shriveled hand clutches
a bare cane and she perches
like a pigeon on a nubbed
log as she drags in shallow
breaths from heavy air.

Street Woman

Perched on a white pail
puffing on a cigarette,
exhaling a thin grey
whisper of smoke.

Her proud demeanor says it all:
"I trusted the world to be
warm. A red blanket of hope
now rests on the lap
of my body & soul."

I Love to a Degree

"I love, to a degree,"
   a friend once said

Today I am plagued with the thought
   of the clutter I add to earth

I don't have the freedom of a bird
   or the courage of the freed Flaco, famed

Owl, sadly doomed by his failure to sense
   poison in a rat

The way of the world is bizarre,
   not something to belittle or disregard

Who can prepare for the ins and outs? To be free? To be doomed?
   Survival, a rare trait that despots cultivate and master best

To me the squirrels in Central Park seem free,
   swinging and scrambling up trunks of trees

And they warn their kin with screeching sounds
   (keening) when raptors approach

Thank our goodness that no human has thought yet
   of scattering toxic peanuts on their turf

Tactics of dictators, civilized and in the wild, come and go
      Perhaps I divine comfort in believing there is always more

To discover from the better core of minds
      As I think about the clutter in my life and the world

I note that to "a degree" I find order in a ray of love
      that beams from the eyes of a friend.

The End Is an Entity

The end is an entity that often
spells something negative,
an absence of what came before.

Yet, the end of pain is a positive,
the end of torture too of course.
But the end of romance often portends

Anger and yet why not embrace what came before,
the richness of togetherness, of sharing that evolved
into something else: the peeling of an onion

That got us to the core. Now a separateness
from one to two entities, a division of sorts,
where on the authentic shore, there is always more.

OBSTACLES

Near Escape

My first psychoanalyst, Dr. Renatus Hartogs*

You are old Hitler, trying
        to convince me
of your good qualities.
        You keep an orange beetle
with black spots
        tied with a key
at your bedside.
        You don't feed it
anymore.

You are a gravedigger
        removing a solid slab
from my grave
        in an underground cemetery.
You disinter my body,
        shuffle papers and declare
you are confused by your findings.

In my dream you own
        a toy store,
and I am another nested
        Russian doll, opening:
blonde to brunette fairy queen,
        a contradiction you point
out like the apple, you think
        I may have poisoned.

You are an old toad, creeping
        out of dark recesses,
waddling in thick mud.

     You emerge warty with forty
years of plumbing oceans,
        donned in the best
underwater equipment.

Hitler, gravedigger, toy store owner, toad,
        you wrap yourself in the cape of
a psychoanalyst's skin.

In my confusion, my poem
        writes the road to escape,
and I run from your demonic clutches.

I was a patient of Dr. Hartogs's for almost a year. Our sessions in his office on Madison Avenue lasted from 15 to 30 minutes. He explained that the time varied depending on how many patients he had waiting to see him. He charged $1/minute.

Dr. Renatus S. Hartogs, a 66-year-old psychiatrist, was directed by a jury in State Supreme Court . . . to pay $350,000 in damages to a woman who accused him of inducing her to enter a sexual relationship with him during the course of her therapy . . . for 14 months in 1969 and 1970.
        —*The New York Times,* March 20, 1975

Marianne, the Octopus and History

Conversation from 81st to 74th St.

On our chilly walk down Central Park West
last night under the moon, past the Museum
of Natural History now devoid of the bold
bronze statue of Theodore Roosevelt on horseback,

Marianne remarks how sad that now
our country seems to disown its history.

Like the Chinese, I say, remembering my travels
in China where I noted that entire ancient cities
were torn down and buried.

I wonder what it means that we've become
like the Chinese, disavowing history? I query.

I guess we'll wait and see, Marianne dismisses.
Then she speaks about a TV show she watched
last night about octopuses. She learned that
females devour their partners after they mate.

How odd, I say. I never knew that.

Not all of them, Marianne consoles.
Just one variety.

Oh, that's a relief, I answer.
But how does she kill him?

Like a pragmatist, she reports,
I guess she eats him.

Like a pathologist searching
for the cause of death, I ask,
but how does she murder him?

I guess she strangles him, Marianne says.
They have a lot of legs, you know.

Oh, I sigh. I guess that explains it.
Then I hum to myself, realizing that
we have not explained anything at all.

Bombast

One has great thoughts
(like saving the Universe)

Some thoughts provoke until they balk
and shrivel like crushed mollusks

on a shore of dry pebbles.

Thought Train

Obsessive thinking:
the same thoughts
twirl like hamsters
racing and whirling on
black, narrow rings.
Over and over, a cheerleader's
baton spins. This side? That?
No, I won't wear this hat, this
crown of wicked thorns
that pinch and pierce
as the rim of steel encircles
and tightens around one ear,
to be worn until perhaps a pill
will still the noise of this train
loose on its useless tracks.

Itch of Impatience

Impatience is an irritation
that tickles my brain
in an annoying vein.
No medication quells
the itch that dwells
in the recesses of my mind.

What then to do with the twitch
but to shut it off with a mindful swish.
Or spend time in a quiet place, where I go
to uplift, to meditate, reach mindless bliss.

Iron Grid

Poetry whizzes all around me.
I am surrounded by sounds of poetry.
Then why, oh why, does it take me so long
to hear it? Is it that I'm bound
by some odd force that fastens
me to an iron grid that won't
allow the air around to sing?

Repetition

Is simply what is happening, what can
or cannot be planned: why she married
on Mulberry or why he resides in France.

Repetition is always something
happening: like the orality of your minister
or the mantra of your mate.

She's nothing like a Nicole. He definitely
resembles a Bob and her dog really
has come to meet and match her demeanor.

Theme after theme
what speaks to you
doesn't necessarily answer.

What Game Is It

Play is all there is
when the brain can't spell well.
In the play I find the sand in the pail
on the ocean shore, wherein the beginnings
of us all lie in that silicon stuff of lucid glass
as clear or cloudy as the gods' eyes
whose game it is to keep us guessing.

Octopus Dilemma

Upon reading "Under the Sea, an 'Octopus Garden' Thrives in the Shade of a Hot Spring," The New York Times, *Sunday, August 27, 2023*

They wrap their protoplasmic legs
around fragile and abundant eggs,
these mothers doomed to die, their sole duty
to beget their offspring, they set to sail upon

The vast and perilous sea; feel the pulse
of the tentacles draped around rock,
the vibrating breath so close to my own
beating heart, a creature I respect.

Unfortunate pulsing mollusk
trapped in a net by slimy bait,
Now life lost. My luscious feast.

Lively animal of the sea tantalizes
with ample brain and twirling feet,
yet I am ruthless: yearn to eat.

To taste a fragment of one appendage
upon my dinner plate: delicately
seasoned, chewy meat.

The dilemma here is monumental!
To see myself so close to cannibal!

Elephant in the Room (or How to Hide a Big Problem in a Small Space)

To poke the elephant or leave her alone?
(After all, elephants are large and mostly silent.
We can do anything, but let's please abstain
from jangling nerves.) In some ways
elephants speak louder with no voice
from distant corners of earth.

They may have to be narcotized
to keep their proper place. When an
elephant awakens, call a therapist
or re-arrange furniture with the gift
of an interior designer.

The elephant dances and the space
shrinks with the pachyderm's wild gyrations.
A cage may be required but please
leave the firemen out of it.

Best to ensnare the phantom
in a net or to search
for an ample carton.

Occupying Spaces

Who knows what
        hides in the corners
or under chairs.
        I would not
believe the boxes
        here and there
shelves, closets
        hidden spaces.

Anything
        can hide or be
hidden from view
        or even visible
to one eye or another
        if only one wants
to see the morass
        of the mess of
objects and things.

I recall the tale
        of a couple who
bought a run-down
        home.
As they remodeled
        they uncovered
the moldy body
        of a woman

stuffed between the wall's layers.
     A crime unsolved, cooled off,
now resolved.
          But the husband, murderer
          had died years ago.

Oh think of the spaces occupied,
     together or alone.

Being Ghosted

I've been ghosted and I must pick
up the slack, crossing off the names
of those who have shucked me off.
My brain will tidy up the matter
with the intellectual broom of the mind
janitor sweeping the hallways clean.

Sax Player in Pandemic

Early morning in Central Park

Through the trees, the sax player
catches my gaze, and under dark glasses
glowers at me from his stance on the bridge.
Then, he comes closer, crosses over to stand

beside me near the water and from the bottom
of this throat, coarse words ring out. "Hey lady,
I'll play if you pay." Startled, I rifle
through my purse and come up a five-spot

and his voice forces, "Thanks."
Then he heads back to his perch on the bridge
plays for a few minutes until he notes
the gaze of another when he again glowers

and stares until more loot appears.
I try to grasp the plight of the sax player—desperation
in this time of pandemic that drains out
the pleasure and beauty of sound.

I dig into my heart to summon empathy,
and fail miserably, the chords of my soul
tempered by his dour demeanor, the joy
soured by misery and dark mood.

The Wolf Is Coming

Marianne clothes herself in old movies
instead of preparing for the inevitability of death.
She fears it like the Wolf who will devour
her whole, as if she is Little Red Riding Hood
walking alone on the path through the woods
with the basket of goodies to take to her sweet
grandmother sick in bed with a heart condition.

But now it is Marianne and I
who have the heart condition.
We are the grandmothers in bed
and the Wolf is about to devour us.
But the real scary question is:
which one of us will He eat first?

MIRACLES

One Day

Silence. All is quiet on the home front.
Then suddenly, flood gates swing open.
Ripe seeds burst out of tight pods.

And then, just as suddenly, I halt
in my tracks, a floundering hippo, stuck.
A breeze rustles my flimsy tail feathers

As if I'm an agile bird in flight, and I join
the motion of the sparkling white sheets
dancing with wind on a loose clothesline.

Circle Poem

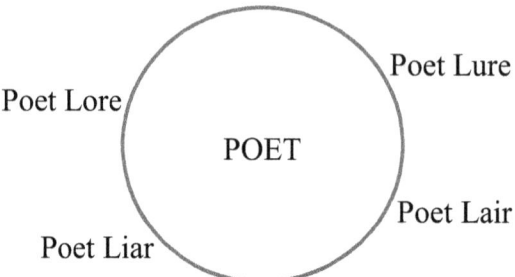

Survival Miracle

On the gratitude list, I cite each daily annoyance that stirs
me and rattles the seismic shifts. We are all in this together,
you know. The AIs are coming to get us. The psychoanalysts
tell me to cope. The surgeons tell me to excise it. My housekeeper
tells me to sew the tear in my slip and repair the hole in the
bathtub. "You could sink to China and then you'd be irretrievable,"
she says. Therein lies the goal. The same one every day no matter
what one's nationality or country: to stay above the clanks
and boards of each sinking ship.

Hurdle On

Every day a new hurdle
to define, then climb
not to despair but take
within a hair of being.
It is my quandary to tarry
and hope that an alternate
angle reveals a novel answer
to this never-ending series
of hurdles that my friends,
the turtles, with aplomb
and long-life, cope, lumber, master.

Hot Flash

A hot flash is not a hot dance
nor a ride on a bare horse
or a sip of chocolate sauce.

This red flush is like a flash in the pan
that reminds us that what was once,
is no longer at hand.

Musician

*Composed following an afternoon spent
with the New York Philharmonic*

What is ticking inside the musician's head,
years of training, playing, learning
the notes, the rote of it all. And I look
on admiring, enthralled by the skill
that given another lifetime I still
might not master unless my neurons
curl like fish tails, to naturally propel
me forward, to swim in a fluid world,
and flow with rhythm and sound.

In London-Like Fog

At Westbeth,
   old seeing eye dog
      grey with olive eyes
walks like the old master,
   beret-covered head
      under fine, London-like mist.

Walks slowly, steadily
   both almost bent over
      at the neck, like my father
reading the newspaper
   at his feet, perched above
      in cushioned chair.

Dog and master legs are
   oak stumps of
      trees, left topless
after hurricanes tearing
   through Rockland County
      of my youth.

Appendaged, either hair-covered
   or trousered, are obtuse angles
      this dark evening, conjuring
visions of skeletons, even their
   bare bones and ligaments
      give way.

Better Self

Does smartness succor
or mitigate the horror
of a person's character?

Freud and I say "nay."
Character can only be saved
by binding the blinding lights
of insight to the clamors of hindsight.

I also invite Yin and Yang
since Confucius offers the promise that
joining light with dark energies will
unite the suffering of my wayward soul.

Moments with a Leporidae, a Canine and Me

The bunny rabbit stays still on the lawn
        several feet away from us.

I hold the dog steady on his leash.
        Cottontail regards us, assesses

the kindness in the tone of my voice
        praising his white tail and smooth tan fur.

In these quiescent moments, in the presence
        of Canine, Leporidae and Human,

the rabbit senses a sanguine space, and I
        am filled with a sense of beauty and grace.

Daughter with Birds

She has a special way with birds.
She sends them a vibration of love.
If she utters a sound, a whistle,
I haven't heard it. Perhaps they alone
hear her tunes? Perceive some smell?
An odor of a special person who worships
their variegated colors, their wings,
delicate nostrils and fickle appetites? Because
they gather to alight on her open palm,
peck peanuts and sunflower seeds. She thrills
in satisfying cardinals, doves, chickadees.
Her patience astounds, the quiet fortitude
she extends to them and grants reluctantly
to a select cadre of us fortunate humans.

Alchemist Artist

Turning junk into art:
I think about it.
Imagination leaping

At the sight of the pile
of childhood relics:
the rusted red bike, the broken hoe.

With hands and brain cells toiling,
seeking that mysterious key that will
turn old fabric to inviting form.

Fashioning art is
imagining how any object
can morph to new-fangled gold.

Pathway of Words

Let's talk about the pathways of words:
one word-mile at a time sketches a map,
the road leading somewhere, although the scribe's
vision may waver in cold, stormy weather.

The words know the way to create the trance in the dance.
Their motion and sounds spell magic and they spurt
the way a whale breaches the surface
for oxygen, or a newborn's first gasp.

Impetus

With dash of color and brush
Van Gogh smashed on canvas
divine green essence of cypress

Muse

I train my muse daily.
Her wings light as a fairy's
so I coax and treat her gingerly
to earn her visits frequently.

How mightily with unpredictability
she alights, and ever too soon
flits away: turns lights out like
a June bug taking off July.

Saving the Orchids

*Dr. C.L. Withner, a renowned orchidologist dedicated
his life to studying and conserving orchids.*

He worked as a savior,
salvaging dried orchids
reviving roots and leaves
semi-dead stems and blooms.

> Would that we each aspire
> to a lofty mission, set our sights
> on an opening of blue sky.

If each of us were nurtured from our beginning,
a word or a kiss or a cuddle could hike us
above the grime and agony of our being.

> We, too, could vibrate, thrive,
> each like a bud on the stem
> of a cherished plant, like the orchid.

Common Sense

Common Sense does not
leap from weeds or trees.
No one really knows
which brain cells
feed this mysterious sense
that too rarely surfaces
at command. Not like
a well-trained dog,
though canines may have
more feel for it than some of us
poor folk lost in the dark
like when to stretch for the carrot
adds up to common sense:
it is what we need
but won't stretch to get.

> ... some people said they would stick to a compromised [web]site because they had put so much time and effort into their presence on it—a classic sunk-cost fallacy.
> —*The Wall Street Journal,* Sept. 28, 2023, R8

> *So at 10:00 pm/you're standing here /with your hand in the air,/cold but too stubborn to reach/into your pocket for a glove, cursing/the freezing rain . . .*
> —Deborah Garrison, *Worked Late on a Tuesday Night*

Expectations

Who sets up what or creates
the expectations of what?

The eternal dilemma
that smooths or toughens

Souls, young and open
to the wide expanse

Of expectation that adds or detracts
from an array of adventures

That rewards with some luscious flesh
or hurls toward disappointment

Regret akin to empty shells
on the shores that echo loss

Passing

I speak of those who have passed
with a spontaneous tone I never knew before,
sounds as natural as logs seep
with rainwater into bogs
where beavers frolic
among a mound of rocks
as if they will never stop
even if earth dries up.

Exit

At my death, please don't mourn me.
    I have led a full life. I ask nothing more
from earth as I pass. You have been generous.
    I don't crave attention. I will spread my wings
and beg to spare the world of pollution's detritus.
    By which I mean I wish to sail away, unannounced,
silent as a cloud floating, released
    into nothingness, which is everything I ask.

A Meditation on Ruth's Cradle

Ruth B. Simon, seismologist and mother of five (1917–2006)]

Impermanent alas are all formations.
    —Buddhist saying

1
I wish I knew the story behind the acquisition
of Ruth's cradle. Solid oak unadorned
with a tall headboard, and long sides
bound by tongues fit into grooves.

I would have asked the carpenter
Why so long? An odd length for a child.
Would the tree have whispered?
"Take the glory in my height of wood."

2
Decades ago, the cradle held a child
in the bedroom of a townhouse. The mother
glows and rocks him and he's soothed.
A handsome toe head, blonde and bare.
He will grow into a good length for a man.

Prouder Ruth has never been to give birth
in her bedroom, then to rock him
in solid oak and cradle in bare flesh
tight to her nurturing breast.
Strong arms will hold child after child.

From the womb, a first home,
then shoved into the treacherous world.
The cradle rocks to soothe,
solid wood against soft flesh.

3
A cradle is not a canoe.
Earth and sea roil in their unique way.
How lucky was Moses to be
plucked from the stream where he
could have perished in a cradle-basket
seeping water. Where would civilization be?
And where I without Ruth's fertility?

From the Mesopotamian cradle
five civilizations sprouted. From Ruth's
cradle, five grew into strong people.

4
With babies grown, Ruth moved on
from cradle rocking, morphed to seismologist,
a scientist traversing the globe
mastering patterns of the quaking world.

The globe too is a cradle. So, it is not
unnatural that from cradles, Ruth
would grapple with quakes
arising above earth's molten core.

5
When in '89, a gigantic quake rocked
San Francisco, Ruth trembled too,
fearing the enormity of tremors
she hadn't grasped before.

Damage shook leaves and tore up trees
by roots, dying as they faced the sun
a wild and frightening scene. Boughs broke.
Babies were thrown to rocking ground.

6
A paradox troubles me now: how hard
wood supports soft flesh, and cradle
      songs both soothe and rattle.

      Boughs break
      And babies fall to the ground.

All things arise and pass away,
even trees, even lives.

7
Yet Ruth plowed on, aiming to foretell
the tumult above earth's core.

Although the cradle stood in Ruth's home
passed on too late to hold a grandchild.
I wonder if she kept it to remind
of a body's fertility, long past.

All things arise and pass away.
Cradles rock over quaking earth.

8
If I could, I would replant the roots
from which Ruth's cradle was hewn.
From the tree, I surmise a whisper,
"Return me to the ground where
tall and proud I once stood,
a glorious height of wood."

9
For her last home, Ruth chose neither
ground nor wood, but clay vessels
to hold ashes laden with memories
living on at five dispersed residences.

10
Cradles rock over quaking earth.
All things arise and pass away.
Even trees, even lives, the Buddhists
chant and sing to cradle-earth.

Learning to Love the Old

The wrinkles in the withering, like a Shar Pei dog.
The motif of motion, the creaking of a warped door.
The sheen of skin, weathering like her leather bag.
The hum of the heart, hesitating . . . steps in the dark.
The liver in the gut, lingering, the robin dazed on a frozen lawn.
The brain in the skull, blundering, through the dense snowstorm.
The fingers failing a fine tuning, a pianist lacking good form.
The toes curling, missing their grounding, the pitchfork, worn.
She resolves to gather up her parts into a neat parcel and,
listening to the night's silence, swim to the far shore.

About the Author

Jane Simon has ascended the ladder from pathology to psychiatry to poetry. She is the author of *Who's Ever Enough* and *A Toolbox of Blogs: Integrating Psyche and Society,* as well as two illustrated books, *The Cabala of Animals* and *A Toolbox of Paradox*. Her poetry has appeared in the *Arizona Quarterly, Black Buzzard Review, Columbia Poetry Review,* and *The Ravens Perch,* among others. An alumna of Barnard College and Temple University School of Medicine, she lives and practices psychiatry in Manhattan.

www.ingramcontent.com/pod-product-compliance
Lightning Source LLC
Chambersburg PA
CBHW031637160426
43196CB00006B/453